Indians of the Great Plains

Linhoff

W9-ALU-504

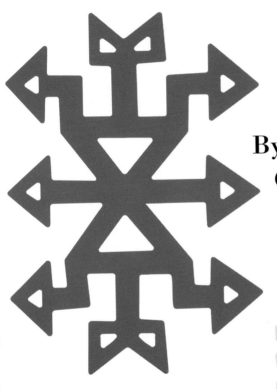

By Mira Bartók and
Christine Ronan

GoodYearBooks
An Imprint of ScottForesman
A Division of HarperCollins*Publishers*

**United
States**

Before 1850, the Plains Indians
lived on the open grasslands of
the midwestern United States.

The prairie was rich with wildlife.

The Indians traveled across it
hunting buffalo and other animals.

Today, the
Plains Indians
live in cities
and towns,
and on farms,
ranches, and
reservations.

The people who live on ranches raise
animals. They are grateful to these
animals for their gifts of life.

Some Indians thank the animals by making beautiful objects, designs, and clothing.

They carry
on ancient
traditions
in this way.

The Pow-wow
is a celebration
of Indian
culture, both
old and new.

People
come
together
from all over
to dance,
drum and
trade goods.

The beat of the drum is the
driving force for the dancers.

A Pow-wow is a great place to make new friends!

Ancient traditions are passed
down from elders.

It is up to children to bring together the old ways and the new.